Time Management

Efficiency Techniques For Attaining Enhanced Outcomes With Reduced Exertion And Optimize Your Schedule To Reclaim The Joys Of Life

(Initiate An Enterprise Despite An Overwhelming Schedule Through The Implementation Of Productivity Practices)

Bogumir Wanta

TABLE OF CONTENT

Prioritize Your To-Do List Every Morning And Review Your Day Every Night.. 1

Begin Each Day With A Well-Structured Agenda....22

Manage External Time Wasters......................................28

Self-Motivation And Cultivating Enhanced Behavioral Patterns 54

Common Errors In Time Management Frequent Pitfalls In Managing Time Typical Mistakes In Time Management Widespread Errors In Time Management 69

Alter Your Perspective On Time And Your Approach To Work. 90

Time Management Techniques.................................... 107

Maintaining One's Motivation Amidst Unfavorable Circumstances 117

Commencing Your Work: 127

Reward Yourself 138

Spending Free Time Passionately 145

Avoiding Procrastination 162

Prioritize Your To-Do List Every Morning And Review Your Day Every Night

I have intentionally saved the most outstanding aspect for the final presentation.

This represents the final approach, which is the most viable strategy as it can be implemented on a daily basis. I will now present a straightforward Daily Routine that is to be performed each morning and evening. This Daily Routine ensures optimal utilization of each day. It additionally ensures that you are engaged in an ongoing, unceasing process of maintaining consistent personal growth.

It is imperative that you engage in a regular practice of reviewing your daily goals or To Do list each morning in a diligent manner. Subsequently, you are advised to establish a hierarchy of your daily objectives by implementing the widely recognized A-B-C system employed within the realm of time management.

The procedure is exceedingly uncomplicated: designate a letter (A, B, or C) to each task corresponding to the significance of that task. (For individuals who tend to be more active during nighttime, it is possible to perform this activity prior to retiring for the night.) By following this approach, one gains the advantage of awakening with a clear understanding of the tasks that must be accomplished on that particular day.

The activities designated as A tasks are the ones that you are required to complete for the day.

Designate the highest priority task of the day as "A1".

This is of utmost importance and should be given highest priority throughout the day. If you successfully accomplish the A1 task, you can confidently conclude that you have had a day of prosperity.

The secondary task will be categorized as A2, followed by A3, and subsequently.

Items that warrant a B classification are those that ought to be done.

They shall be categorized as B1, B2, B3, and subsequent designations.

Actions that may be undertaken receive a C categorization. These activities hold a relatively lower level of importance compared to A or B activities. It would be greatly appreciated if you could kindly undertake these tasks for the day. These low priority activities will be classified as C1, C2, C3, and so forth.

"Presented herewith are the regulations governing this Daily Routine:

Exercise discretion while choosing your A1 activity, taking into consideration the 80/20 Principle.

Ensure that your A1 task is unequivocally the utmost priority that you can devote your attention to throughout the day.

Give priority to completing your A1 activity.

Making the completion of your A1 activity the foremost priority of the day is highly recommended.

Please dedicate ample time and allocate the necessary resources to successfully accomplish task A1, even if it entails omitting the completion of all other tasks, namely A, B, and C, from your agenda. The rationale behind this is that the completion of your A1 activity signifies the utmost accomplishment and triumph you can attain on that particular day.

Following the completion of A1, commence with the execution of A2.

Complete the remaining A activities (A3, A4, etc).

Only once that criterion is met can you begin working on B activities.

Initiate C activities solely upon the conclusion of all A and B activities.

Conclude each day by conducting a thorough examination of the events that transpired.

Reflect upon your actions and pose the question, "In what ways did I exhibit proficiency?" Enumerate all the achievements you have accomplished throughout the day.

Afterward, introspect and inquire, "In what manner could I have improved?" Make a written record of the modifications you would make if presented with the opportunity to relive the day.

Implement the knowledge acquired on the subsequent day.

Efficiently modify and enhance your daily practices, systems, procedures, and the like.

Please ensure that this cycle is repeated on a daily basis.

If you commit to this practice for the next 90 days, you will witness a significant enhancement in the overall quality of your life.

Please ensure that you remain safe and I wish you the best of luck in your endeavors.

Adrian Knight

One task that can be automated presently

Identify a particular aspect of your daily routine that consumes a significant amount of your time, and automate its processes using robotics. Taking everything into account, would you be capable of scheduling an upcoming invoice payment instead of handling it manually?

Here are some ideas:

1. Subsequently arranged automated payment for the service invoice.

2. Submit your lease payment in advance by a few days or weeks to preemptively address the matter, thus avoiding the need to contemplate it in the future.

3. Respond to two or three supplementary messages within the course of today.

Eliminating a single task can consistently free up a few minutes of additional energy... that undergoes a transformation to span several hours or days on an annual basis.

Time-Saving Tip #4: Avoiding the Use of Snooze Function

In reference to a clock, promptly awaken when the morning timer sounds. I understand that it may appear more convenient to wake up if you consistently hit the snooze button and allow the alarm to go off repeatedly at regular intervals. However, does an extra 9 minutes of rest truly hold any substantial value?

From my perspective, if one were to enter a pool contaminated with a virus, it would be prudent to promptly immerse oneself rather than gradually testing the waters by first dipping a toe, then a toe, and eventually a foot. It's torment that way.

Complete the task promptly and regain consciousness. If you experience difficulty arising in the morning, it would be beneficial to retire to bed at an earlier hour, create a tranquil sleeping environment, invest in a superior mattress, or engage in physical activity throughout the day. In such a manner, you will become fatigued come nightfall. It is highly advisable not to activate the snooze feature when the alarm sounds in the morning.

Never Wait... Ever!

You should refrain from utilizing the term 'wait' under any circumstances in your daily existence.

I was made aware of this during a previous Mark Joyner interview several years ago. No individual within the office of Mark Joyner was granted permission to employ the phrase 'stand by' ... Given that the act of holding up signifies a lack of action. I possess the ability to ascertain your thoughts... Each and every one of Mark's employees would replace the phrase "stand by!" with an additional word. Your assertion would be accurate. When one intends to convey the signal 'pause' ... you stop briefly. I am prohibited from using that term. Take a moment to contemplate the reasoning behind your decision to wait, if you will.

It would be difficult for you to fathom the actions of those individuals whom you do not wish to disclose, if you had the chance to witness them. For example, those individuals who send me the most solicitations for assistance, or inquire within a couple of minutes of making such requests... employ specific lexical choices in their language.

The most renowned example I have come across is the term 'work.' Unfortunately, this content proves to be ineffective... The functionality of the framework in this digital publication did not align with my requirements. For them, success hinges on achieving substantial victories or facing utter failure... It is conceivable that it was successful or unsuccessful.

Unconsciously, they are contemplating the alternative connotation of the term "work" ... laboring away at something. They embarked upon this endeavor... Moreover, the content failed to function properly.

Alternatively, convert it into a positive outcome. Instead of the content being ineffective, state... I pursued a series of advancements, both in this regard and in that regard, and this is the outcome that transpired. What other course of action would be advisable for me to explore?

Furthermore, it will never complain. We are all familiar with that particular individual who exhibits a lack of certainty and effectiveness... Additionally, one is consistently discouraged or anxious. They incessantly express discontent about every little thing, and a straightforward approach can be employed to bypass such behavior.

After excluding the term 'stand by' from your vernacular... Make an effort to eradicate discontent as well. It's simple. Should you possess any unfavorable statements, ensure to conclude your assertion with a positive aspect.

As an example, a counterargument could be presented as follows: "There was significant congestion encountered during the journey back home today."

A positive alternative expression would be: "An optimistic perspective on the situation would be: 'Although I encountered traffic during my commute today, I will make a note to take Main Street in the future.' Let us cultivate a serene mindset."

Time-Saving Tip #5: Prioritize Hair Washing During the Evening

It is advisable to cleanse your hair the evening before, particularly if you possess considerably long hair. However, on occasions, I personally opt to wash my hair the preceding night in order to maximize efficiency and minimize time consumption. This is because tending to one's hair in the morning requires additional effort, necessitating an earlier awakening when one is already groggy, inevitably leading to reduced productivity and sluggishness.

If you have the opportunity to cleanse your hair on the previous evening, that implies that you can skip this task the next day, thereby alleviating some of your responsibilities.

Efficiency Tip #6: Incorporate Teeth Brushing into your Shower Routine

Please ensure that you clean your teeth either before or during your shower. Ensure that you possess a separate toothbrush and a distinct receptacle of toothpaste designated for use in the shower.

During the time you place your trust in the efficacy of the cleanser or while you apply soap to your body, it is advisable to concurrently devote attention to the brushing of your teeth with the other hand. It is an additional effective technique for accomplishing two tasks simultaneously while optimizing time.

It may necessitate a certain amount of instruction. It could potentially be deemed imprudent to engage in the act of brushing one's teeth during the course of showering, solely for the purpose of economizing merely 1 or 2 minutes of time on a daily basis.

Efficiency Tip #7: Prepare Twice the Amount of Food

Cook twofold how much food you really want. Is it not the case that prior to commencing work, as a customary practice, if one is preparing dinner, they are most likely also preparing breakfast? In such circumstances, it would be prudent to consider preparing a greater quantity of food than initially intended, storing the surplus in a Tupperware container, and subsequently reheating it on the following day.

There is no need to undergo the additional inconvenience associated with cooking once more. Simply place the food item on the stove or in the microwave, and within a short period of time, your breakfast, lunch, or any other meal will be adequately heated and fully prepared for consumption.

Time-Saving Technique #8: Ensure Prompt Dish Cleanup

It is important to avoid leaving dirty dishes out as it can significantly waste time. I acknowledge that especially during the early hours, you may feel inclined to set a plate aside. Rinse it with some water and place it in the dishwasher.

It is permissible to use the dishwasher while you are working to ensure that, later in the evening, when you are fatigued from the day, you will not be inclined to leave dirty dishes in the sink. Rather than allowing this problem to accumulate, it is advised to never leave unwashed dishes unattended.

Address it during the evening hours, or prior to commencing one's professional duties... Clean the dishes beforehand and place them in the dishwasher, thereby alleviating any further concerns.

Time-saving tip number nine: Consistently store keys in a designated location.

Consistently maintain the practice of storing your keys in a consistent location, ensuring that such location is represented by a designated receptacle, a specific tabletop, or even within the confines of your trousers, so as to preserve uniformity. By following this approach, you can ensure that you are not tardy, hastily departing the premises, and having to search your residence for the whereabouts of your keys. Please place your keys in the designated location.

Efficiency Enhancer #10: Utilizing Audio Books During Your Commute

Ultimately, once you have departed from the premises, it is recommended that you engage in the practice of consuming audio books while undertaking your daily commute to the workplace. Alternatively, should you choose to engage in physical exercise at the gym prior to commencing work, the suggestion is to immerse yourself in the auditory experience provided by a book on your portable iPod device rather than engaging in conventional reading. I acknowledge that one may engage in perusing books for relaxation; however, it would be a more efficient allocation of your time to attentively engage with an accompanying audio material while performing menial tasks such as driving or exercising.

Research findings indicate that actively engaging with audio books during extended periods of a typical commute can be equated to the educational value gained from attending a two-year community college program. You may employ this ample amount of free time to acquire a new language or develop a new skill.

Begin Each Day With A Well-Structured Agenda

A plan is a strategic framework or navigational tool that enables individuals to stay aligned and directed towards accomplishing their objectives. In the absence of a well-devised strategy, individuals are prone to becoming entangled in diversions, ultimately engaging in activities unintended or unplanned for.

Please make a determination regarding the tasks you wish to accomplish today and allocate a dedicated time slot for their completion. If a task needs to be done at a specific time, you can put it on your calendar. Alternatively, you should commence your day by prioritizing the most crucial task. It is important to bear in mind that when planning tasks, it is advisable to allocate adequate buffer time between them to accommodate potential delays. It is advisable to avoid scheduling tasks consecutively.

Habit 2 - Entrust tasks to others to the greatest extent feasible

Do not hesitate to assign tasks to others. As previously mentioned, dedicating your time to significant tasks should be prioritized, as less significant tasks may be effectively delegated to others. It is advisable to delegate tasks to others to the greatest extent possible in order to prioritize and concentrate solely on the most crucial assignments.

Habit 3 ? Efficiently arrange and manage your residential and occupational spaces

Establish order! Establish order! Establish order! This is an extremely significant conduct. Consider the following: If one constantly dedicates substantial time to the task of locating objects, how effective can their overall productivity truly be? What is your reaction when you allocate an hour for the purpose of composing a report, only to devote the initial 15 minutes to preparatory tasks due to the inability to locate either the necessary stationery or crucial information? Maintain a systematic approach to organizing your home and workplace to effortlessly locate items without the need for cognitive effort.

Habit 4 - Eliminate sources of interruption

Please refrain from using the TV, listening to music, accessing web browsers, and using phones while focusing on a critical task. If it is unnecessary to utilize the Internet, one may opt to disconnect it. As I have previously stated, I consistently disconnect from the Internet while engaging in writing activities, thereby enhancing my ability to concentrate on the task at hand.

Habit 5 ? Determine your most efficient time frame.

As an individual who prefers to rise early, I have observed that the early hours of the day enable me to execute my tasks with heightened efficiency. However, this does not encompass all individuals as certain individuals possess a predisposition towards being active during nighttime hours. Identify the period of maximum productivity and allocate that time specifically to significant tasks, making them the utmost priority. Upon awakening in the morning, I consistently engage in the act of writing before commencing any physical exercise.

Habit 6 - Establish a predetermined timeframe for the completion of a task.

It is a common occurrence for individuals to remain unaware of their true capabilities until they consciously venture beyond the confines of their comfort zone. The word "deadline" may invoke a sense of pressure, but failing to establish a predetermined timeframe for a task's completion can lead to an unnecessarily prolonged process. In the absence of a set deadline, it becomes effortless to defer the task, as one might casually remark, "I can attend to it at a later time."

Manage External Time Wasters

External factors imposed by individuals and circumstances outside of your control may exert an impact on the allocation of your time. One can reduce or eliminate the amount of time allocated to these activities by implementing a few straightforward recommendations as outlined below.

Meetings

Approximately one-fourth to half of managerial time is allocated to attending meetings. These encounters can take the form of individualized meetings, spontaneous interactions in the hallway, or more official gatherings conducted in an office or designated meeting space.

Regrettably, a significant portion, equal to or exceeding 50%, of meeting time is squandered. Meetings expend considerable amounts of time and yield minimal enduring value. Nevertheless, meetings also serve as a crucial tool in management and necessitate efficient utilization.

Estimate the expenses associated with the meeting

Please ensure that you possess a valid rationale for contacting or participating in any gathering. Regard every meeting as a strategic investment, one that incurs expenses in terms of managerial and staff time, as well as wages.

Take the combined hourly pay of the people in those meetings and realize that you need to get a return on your investment of this amount of money.

If a gathering comprises a total of ten individuals, each earning an average hourly wage of $50, then the monetary commitment for a one-hour meeting amounts to $500. If an individual sought approval to allocate a budget of $500 towards a particular initiative, it would be important for you to ascertain the anticipated value and benefits that the company would derive from this expenditure. It is advisable to carefully consider it for a period of time before granting approval. You may even request additional information and specifics prior to feeling sufficiently confident in authorizing an expenditure of this magnitude.

Approach every meeting with equal importance and consideration.

Avoid unnecessary meetings. Continuously consider the necessity of convening a meeting. Whenever one determines that a meeting is unnecessary, it becomes imperative to abstain from convening said meeting. If it is not necessary for you to be present at the meeting, then please refrain from attending.

If you are in charge of arranging the meeting, consider determining the individuals who are crucial to the proceedings, and extend invitations exclusively to those individuals. Kindly avoid extending invitations to individuals who do not possess a genuine necessity to attend, solely for the purpose of appeasing their self-esteem or sense of importance.

Prepare an Agenda

Ensure a formalized agenda is created for each meeting, and consistently adhere to it. Arrange the items on the agenda in order of priority, giving precedence to the most significant ones, in the event that time becomes insufficient.

As the facilitator of the meeting, it is your responsibility to steer the conversation in the right direction and ensure that each agenda item is thoroughly addressed and concluded before proceeding to the next.

Commence and conclude your meetings punctually. If there are individuals who consistently arrive late, it may be worth contemplating the action of securing the entrance shortly following the designated commencement time. Another approach could be to proceed with the meeting under the assumption that the individual who arrives late will not be joining, and commence accordingly.

Once the meeting commences, please ensure there are no disruptions while you are in attendance. In Marshall Goldsmith's highly acclaimed literary work titled "What Got You Here Won't Get You There," he asserts that one of the most substantial deficiencies in leadership lies in the inclination to exert excessive control over meetings attended by the leader's subordinates.

Due to your authoritative role, everyone pays heed when you communicate. Over the course of time, individuals acquire the ability to refrain from verbal expression or interruption, opting instead to allow you to expound upon any topic of your choosing for an extended duration.

Ask More Questions

When attending a meeting, adopt the behavior of the astute and judicious owl which possesses two ears and one mouth. Employ a balanced measure of listening and speaking. In order to actively engage in the discussion, it is advisable to inquire further and attentively observe while speaking sparingly, or make valuable inputs to the established objectives.

Utilize a meeting as a platform to extract the utmost intellectual contributions from each individual present, an accomplishment that cannot be attained if one monopolizes the conversation. The most optimal and effective meetings consist of standing-up, if not seating arrangements. You may consider convening such a meeting, potentially in your office, where attendees remain standing - and any pertinent matters are addressed promptly and concisely to enable a swift return to work for everyone involved.

It is relatively straightforward to convene such a meeting. Given the constraints of limited time and recognizing the busy schedules of all individuals involved, I propose that we convene a brief and concise meeting. In doing so, we will be able to address all necessary aspects and expedite our return to work."

Considering individuals' typically busy schedules, one can observe that this particular meeting is greatly valued by your staff members, provided it is arranged at an appropriate time and venue.

Telephone

The telephone can serve as a highly proficient servant, or conversely, a formidable dominator - particularly if one feels obligated to respond promptly to every call. In order to optimize productivity, it is imperative to position the telephone appropriately, so as to avoid becoming subordinate to anyone who dials your number.

The most effective approach to managing your telephone communications is to prioritize call screening for all incoming calls, if feasible. Alternatively, please set your mobile phone to silent mode and allow incoming calls to be directed to your voicemail. There are minimal instances where it would be necessary to delay attending to calls or messages until a more opportune time.

One of the factors contributing to our increasing susceptibility to the lure of distraction is our innate sense of curiosity. We are unable to refrain from pondering the identity of the sender of the message, or the individual situated at the opposite side of the telephone.

The sole means of resisting such temptations that lead to distractions is to shut off the phone entirely, ensuring that you do not even perceive its audible signals. On occasions when you have scheduled meetings with your staff, subordinates, superiors, or clients, kindly request that your phone calls be placed on hold. Please switch off your mobile device.

Allow no interruptions whatsoever. Rarely is there something of such significance that it cannot be postponed.

Engaging in a ten-minute uninterrupted dialogue with another person is more fruitful than a thirty or forty-minute conversation that is frequently interrupted by phone calls being answered. You may contact individuals at a later time.

Bunch Your Calls

If you require to conduct a sequence of telephone communications throughout the day, it is advisable to conduct them simultaneously.

Allocate a substantial portion of your schedule during which you can eliminate all other forms of disturbance and solely dedicate it to placing phone calls to the individuals mentioned on your roster. Record the name, contact number, and topic of each individual whom you are required to contact.

Avoid Telephone Tag

Make every effort to avoid engaging in a game of telephone tag.

Arrange telephone appointments with the same level of attention and preparation as you would when organizing in-person meetings within the office. When initiating a phone call with individuals, kindly provide a designated time and contact number at which you would be accessible. It is expected that you be present in your office or accessible by telephone during business hours in order to promptly address any incoming calls.

Utilize the telephone as a valuable tool for business purposes. Efficiently maneuver between telephone calls. Get straight to the point. Exhibit politeness and amiability while maintaining a professional demeanor and a focus on achieving desired outcomes.

The greater your level of precision and organization regarding the timing and subject matter of your telephone conversation, the higher your efficiency will be, resulting in increased productivity during each call.

Batch Your Tasks

Batching your tasks entails the act of performing similar activities during concurrent sessions.

There is a learning curve associated with every task or endeavor. When consecutive instances of similar or identical tasks are performed, the learning curve enables a reduction in the amount of time needed to complete each task by as much as 80% by the time the fifth identical task is accomplished.

As an illustration, when engaging in written correspondence such as letters or email responses, it is customary to collate and address them collectively, completing them concurrently. You batch your telephone calls and return them all in a row. When conducting interviews with multiple individuals, it is advisable to sequentially interview them, one after the other.

Engage in concurrent execution of comparable tasks rather than fragmenting your efforts across different moments.

Utilize Email as a Tool

Your approach to managing your email correspondence will greatly influence the amount of time you have at your disposal.

There exist individuals who are ensnared by the bondage of electronic communication. They possess a bell that sounds every time a new email is received, prompting them to promptly redirect their attention to their inbox in order to inspect the message. As a result, they frequently shift their focus away from their most critical tasks, resulting in a decline in momentum, clarity, and productivity upon returning to them.

In his acclaimed publication titled "The 4-Hour Workweek," Tim Ferris provides an account of his transformation from being excessively burdened by his email for twelve to fourteen hours per day, to achieving full mastery over the process.

Initially, he made the determination to exclusively respond to his email on two occasions throughout the day, precisely at 11 AM and 4 PM. Subsequently, he transitioned from responding twice daily to responding only once a day. Subsequently, it will occur once a week.

His efficiency, effectiveness, and productivity demonstrated marked improvement even when responding to emails on a weekly basis.

They Can Wait

Certain individuals who demonstrate high levels of productivity possess innate or reflexive tendencies to promptly respond to their electronic mail. It is phrased as follows: 'I am only able to respond to my email twice per day due to the demands of my hectic schedule.' In the event that you have forwarded me an email, I shall respond to you at the earliest opportunity. In the event of an emergency, please dial the provided number and communicate with the designated individual."

A journalist who had a hectic schedule recounted the account of undertaking a journey to Europe spanning a duration of two weeks. His email remained inaccessible throughout the entire duration. Upon his arrival, he was greeted with an accumulation of over 700 messages awaiting his attention.

He was aware that it would require a substantial amount of time, potentially spanning multiple days, to thoroughly review and respond to 700 emails. With a composed demeanor, he drew a profound breath and pressed the command labeled "erase all". He stated, "I decline the role of servitude to any individual who dispatches me an electronic message with the expectation of prompt response." Moreover, in the event that any of these emails hold significance, the sender will surely dispatch them once more."

And his assertion was accurate; a significant majority of the emails he erased were never duplicated, and the ones he deleted which held significance were resent within a brief timeframe.

Opt for a resolution to refrain from permitting your email to dominate your existence, akin to a scenario where the subordinate becomes the master. Conversely, exercise self-control in employing electronic mail as a professional instrument.

Please provide prompt and concise responses. Please limit the frequency of checking your email to twice a day or even less frequently. Moreover, it would be advantageous to refrain from using your email during the weekends and allocate more time to be spent with your family and friends, or to engage in personal endeavors.

The positive development is that it is highly unlikely that you will ever overlook a critical message. There are only a limited number of occurrences that are of such urgency that they cannot be postponed for another day or two.

Read Faster, Remember More

The modern professional is frequently engaged in the consumption of an extensive volume of textual content, encompassing emails, reports, news articles, business materials, magazine features, and various informational sources. In order to achieve success in the present day, it is imperative to ensure that one remains updated with their reading obligations. We reside in a society driven by knowledge, wherein a single pivotal piece of information can swiftly impact both your professional endeavors and decision-making processes.

Exercise discernment in choosing your reading materials. The most efficient time-saving tool in the realm of reading and staying up-to-date is the delete function on your keyboard.

Matters that do not possess immediate significance or relevance to one's personal and professional endeavors.

Learn to Speed-Read

One cannot evade the entirety of incoming information, but one can categorize it and sift through it at a designated time and location that aligns with one's preferences and priorities.

Acquiring the ability to comprehend text at an accelerated pace is an invaluable skill that one should strive to nurture. If you have not previously enrolled in a course on speed reading, it is recommended that you do so. This particular course will enable you to significantly enhance both your reading speed and level of retention, resulting in a threefold increase. The advancements in speed reading techniques are truly remarkable, as individuals have the ability to acquire the skill of reading at a rate of 500 to 1,000 words per minute while maintaining a high level of comprehension.

Bunch Your Reading

When encountering valuable items, summaries, or pieces of information on the Internet, it is advisable to print them out and store them in a physical file or save them in a designated digital folder on your computer for subsequent reading.

Rather than engaging in "task-shifting" - which refers to diverting your attention from the current task at hand to read a recent piece of information - it is recommended to set it aside for later perusal. Upon developing this practice, you will be astounded by the significant increase in your reading capacity and the enhanced level of attentiveness you can dedicate to the material.

With respect to newspapers, one has the option of receiving the most significant information regularly published in newspapers on their computer or alternatively reading the print edition. Regardless of the scenario, swiftly skim the content and focus solely on the information that is pertinent to your needs. In the realm of news reporting, paramount information typically resides within the headline and the initial paragraph. Frequently, it is unnecessary to peruse the entirety of the narrative in order to grasp precisely what transpired.

Read Selectively

Magazines are meticulously created and structured to engage readers, compelling them to peruse each page. This will ensure that you receive optimal exposure to the advertisements featured in the magazines. (It is analogous in the case of newspapers.)

Given this rationale, it is advisable to peruse magazines, journals, newspapers, and newsletters judiciously, limiting your reading to material that is pertinent and significant to your needs.

Review the table of contents and go straight to the articles of interest to your life and work.

A highly effective method for managing printed materials entails the employment of a strategy known as "rip and read." This approach involves extracting the desired articles from the source material, organizing and storing them in a designated file, and subsequently carrying the file for later reference during idle moments.

Exercise due diligence when evaluating books before determining which ones warrant your valuable reading time. One may opt to avail book review services, available both in print and online formats, in order to obtain the most insightful concepts from any literary work within a matter of minutes.

Just Say No

The most efficient approach to minimizing time spent on reading is to deliberately choose not to engage with certain materials. Through a meticulous examination of the preface, table of contents, introduction, author's biography, or index, you may discern that the book or journal lacks significance to your particular interests. In such circumstances, it is recommended to cease reading or completely discard it so as to allocate additional time for matters of greater significance.

Self-Motivation And Cultivating Enhanced Behavioral Patterns

It is essential to maintain your motivation in order to consistently perform at the highest level of productivity. There exists a multitude of factors that one can employ to cultivate self-motivation. A few examples include:

Public Obligation: Upon voluntarily undertaking a task, one incurs a duty towards the public at large to complete said task. Failure to complete the assigned task within the designated timeframe will invariably tarnish your reputation in the eyes of those individuals who rely on your timely delivery. These people could be your boss or any other person that you are accountable to. Hence, it is imperative to regard the public commitment as a significant catalyst propelling one towards the successful completion of said task.

Mitigation of Loss: When engaging in a project, it is imperative to bear in mind that any failure to diligently pursue its completion will result in incurring various forms of loss, whether it be of a financial nature or arising from other consequential outcomes.

Positive Reinforcement: Positive reinforcement can serve as a valuable catalyst for maintaining motivation. Positive reinforcement entails directing your attention towards the task at hand, with the expectation that upon successful completion of said task, you shall be duly rewarded with a specified incentive. You have the option to grant yourself this incentive, or it may be bestowed upon you by your supervisor. This significant element plays a pivotal role in sustaining individuals' motivation towards accomplishing the assigned task.

Operant conditioning involving negative reinforcement entails the application of aversive consequences as a means of discouraging the failure to accomplish a given task. Your superior has the authority to determine the penalty, or alternatively, you may exercise the autonomy to establish a penalty for yourself. The apprehension of retribution serves as a driving force behind an individual's commitment to completing the assigned task.

Using Healthy Competition:

During your time in school, you engaged in competitive activities with fellow students in order to determine the individual who could attain the highest scores. Sports are additionally founded on the principle that either an individual or a collective will emerge as the victor. Competition is an immensely constructive aspect of the workplace, as long as it is established properly and embraced by all participants. As an illustration, one sales team may endeavor to exceed the sales performance of another sales team. The presence of diverse teams provides employees with a benchmark to gauge their accomplishments, thereby encouraging a high level of performance. If one holds the belief that fostering competition within the workplace is possible, it shall be realized that heightened productivity and substantial acquisition of knowledge from fellow colleagues can indeed be achieved.

For optimal success, it is imperative that all individuals demonstrate full commitment and cooperation.

Additionally, it is vital to further develop your proficiency in the art of attentive listening. By collectively gathering ideas on accomplishing tasks, you may uncover exceptional insights from individuals who typically maintain a reserved demeanor. This aspect of effective leadership is of utmost significance. Active listening can be immensely instructive, much like the lessons gleaned from one's own mistakes, provided one is receptive to them. Utilize the collaborative endeavors of the group or team as a valuable platform for generating innovative ideas, ensuring that due recognition is accorded to each contributor.

The omission of this aspect in most literature on productivity can be attributed to the possibility that others may not have encountered the same personal insights and experiences as myself. Upon conducting a comprehensive time and motion study, I have observed that cohesive group efforts yield superior outcomes compared to independent execution of individual tasks. This phenomenon arises due to the inherent tendency of divergent individual responsibilities to result in disparate directions, hindering collective progress.

You have the opportunity to engage in competition with the individual with whom you have the closest working relationship. Participants have the option to engage in the competition either as a collective unit or as individuals paired with another participant, however, it is imperative that they possess a clear understanding of the desired outcome. In a particular office setting, where the email inbox remained perpetually unattended, we assigned the responsibility of devising a resolution to two secretaries with the objective of ensuring that the email inbox was emptied each night prior to departure from work. The benefits derived from such an experience are extensive knowledge, and the young lady who ultimately succeeded in emptying the box was rewarded with a modest prize. Nevertheless, the value she contributed to the company was far greater. She successfully imparted her knowledge to the other secretaries, guiding them in effectively maintaining empty email inboxes. The system she employed proved to be highly efficient.

Formulate templates for the purpose of utilizing them as standardized email responses.

Please provide the response in chronological order, from the earliest to the most recent, and refrain from closing an email until it has been addressed.

Kindly forward those emails requiring attention from others to the appropriate recipient.

Make a determination as to which emails constitute spam and transfer them into the designated spam folder.

Her actions were highly organized and when faced with a significant workload, a substantial portion of it follows a similar pattern. Address each item in a sequential manner, refraining from diverting attention towards other tasks. She was able to visually observe a reduction in the workload, and her rivalry lay in managing the overflowing email inbox rather than perceiving it as a competition against a colleague. One can always envision alternative concepts to contend with. If the duration for responding to an email currently amounts to 15 minutes, gradually reduce this time by one minute, commencing with the subsequent email of 14 minutes, while ensuring that professional conduct is maintained. Utilizing templates will facilitate the completion of this task, as they are provided within the email system and are preloaded with your personalized sign-off signature, along with the majority of the necessary information that you need to communicate to the recipient.

If it is necessary for you to retrieve information, please proceed to do so. It is strongly advised not to procrastinate, as each instance of procrastination results in the loss of approximately 10 minutes of valuable time. This occurs due to the need to reopen the email and ponder over how to appropriately address its contents. Strive for self-improvement in the absence of external competitors, setting the following objectives:

• To ensure that the desk is vacant by the close of business • To achieve a state of desk emptiness by the conclusion of the workday • To make certain that the desk remains unoccupied by the end of the day • To guarantee a desk devoid of any items by the end of business hours

• To ensure all documents are appropriately organized • To maintain a systematic filing system • To arrange everything in a structured manner • To keep all files neatly categorized

- To have responded to each incoming call

- To have replied to each and every email
- To have addressed all incoming emails
- To have responded to all the messages received
- To have dealt with every email adequately

- To ensure that your work schedule for tomorrow is prepared in advance for the morning.

Frequently, I engage in self-competition, which heightens my mindfulness regarding the rapid passage of time. This system can be utilized even within the confines of one's own home to efficiently accomplish routine tasks. In situations where you are obliged to engage in tasks that you find unpleasant, it can be effective to envision yourself as a compensated individual exclusively allocated to perform these activities within a specified time frame. Please bear in mind that once the task is completed, you will have the freedom to engage in other activities. If you fail to complete the task, it may eventually have negative consequences for you. Hence, delaying tasks is not advantageous. Indeed, it significantly compounds the difficulties.

It is advisable for one to wholeheartedly devote oneself to the practice of effective time management and cultivate a consistent routine in this pursuit. To achieve this objective, one can adhere to a series of straightforward and uncomplicated measures.

1. It is advisable to consistently carry a compact notebook in your possession, in which you can diligently document your obligations, impending due dates, as well

as allocate specific time slots for each task. In addition, it is advisable to record the methodologies you are employing as well as other crucial elements such as the tools that will help maintain your motivation.

2. As previously indicated, schedules are highly beneficial in the effective management of time. Consequently, it is advisable to maintain diligent schedules. As your objectives evolve, you have the flexibility to make slight adjustments to those timelines in order to align them with your evolving goals.

3. You are advised to access online resources regarding time management tips and strategies. While it may seem as though reading them is a futile use of your time, the reality is that you will frequently come across techniques and insights that can significantly streamline your efforts.

4. Please bear in mind that work conducted with intelligence and strategic efficiency consistently surpasses strenuous efforts. If a task or activity is consuming a considerable amount of time, there are invariably approaches or methodologies that can substantially reduce its duration. Hence, it is imperative to conduct comprehensive research prior to commencing a task in order to ascertain efficient time-saving strategies. However, it is important to bear in mind that the integrity of the work must not be compromised by the utilization of expedient approaches.

Call to Action

Please procure a sheet of paper and transcribe a comprehensive list of the sequential actions you intend to undertake for the purpose of nurturing self-motivation and cultivating habitual engagement in time management endeavors. Proceed sequentially through the following steps, crossing them out from the list upon their completion.

Common Errors In Time Management Frequent Pitfalls In Managing Time Typical Mistakes In Time Management Widespread Errors In Time Management

There is an absence of personal objectives and a lack of prioritization.

We have previously discussed both of these matters, yet it is pertinent to review them once more for the purpose of reiteration. If you lack a clear vision of your desired future state within the span of six months to one year, it is highly probable that you will find yourself occupying the same position as you currently do when that time frame elapses. We will inevitably reach that seemingly far-off point in the future; the real question is, where will you find yourself when that moment arrives?

Consider an even greater time horizon, such as a decade into the future. Do you possess a personal vision for your life? According to a recent remark made by Brian Tracy, it is our innate nature to succeed; however, in order to achieve success, we must meticulously devise a strategic framework for success, adequately ready ourselves for it, and hold unwavering expectations of victory. Although my interpretation may be slightly altered, I trust that you comprehend the essence of my message. Lacking a well-devised strategy, your ability to accomplish anything of substantial importance will be greatly diminished. If, perchance, you succeed, it will likely be attributed to fortuity, happenstance, or, in particular, if it is a promotion, it will be determined by the desires of others rather than your own aspirations. If you do not possess any explicitly defined personal objectives with a well-defined timeframe, then perhaps it is worth contemplating this matter. Effective time management is facilitated by setting goals, as it provides a clear framework for prioritizing tasks and activities throughout the day. The process of attaining an objective is essentially straightforward, where one endeavors to move from a current position at point A to a desired destination at point B. The journey essentially encompasses the temporal distance separating point A and point B. The duration of time required will evidently vary based on your level of productivity; the more productive you are, the shorter the time span between point A and point B, and conversely, the less productive you are, the longer the interval. The level of productivity you achieve is contingent upon your proficiency in time management. Having a clear objective and a predetermined timeline to accomplish it provides a sense of focus and prioritization, aiding in determining the most worthwhile allocation of time and effort. What is the most impactful or strategic activity that you engage in? Once again, the crux of the matter lies in prioritization. When compiling your daily agenda for the ensuing day, consider deliberating upon the task that possesses the highest potential for yielding substantial advancements. This will assist you in discerning between crucial tasks and those that hold lesser significance.

When it comes to establishing priorities, it is advisable to rely on your intuition. Upon perusing extensive lists, your instincts will naturally guide you towards discerning the relative significance of each item. The most optimal time to carry out tasks that hold significant importance and potential impact is in the early morning. Engaging in such tasks will result in reduced stress and heightened fulfillment throughout the day. Prioritizing the high-impact activities at the beginning of the day will generate a sense of momentum to carry you through the rest of the day. If you succeed in completing that crucial task by midday or early afternoon, you might find yourself effectively accomplishing all those comparatively less significant tasks. If the two priorities were to be reversed and the smaller tasks were tackled first, it would result in increased pressure and burden. Within the recesses of your thoughts, you will maintain cognizance of the consequential endeavor that awaits you later in the day; however, it shall not evoke exhilaration nor imbue you with vitality. Upon completing the aforementioned minor duties, you will not have achieved a significant reduction in stress. Conversely, you will experience heightened stress levels due to restricted time availability for the completion of the crucial task. In addition, it runs the risk of classifying that task as both urgent and important, thus prioritizing it to a level where stress becomes prevalent.

Inadequate management of distractions and procrastination

Distractions can be likened to temporal inefficiencies, occurring sporadically and consuming only a marginal portion of one's time, as they are typically not prolonged in nature. However, it is not solely one distraction that detracts from our time; rather, it is the culmination of numerous distractions experienced throughout the entirety of the day that has this effect. According to research conducted by mind tools, it has been observed that individuals tend to incur a productivity loss of up to two hours per day due to various distractions. Consider the level of productivity that you could have achieved had you been able to reclaim that period of time. Hence, it is imperative to actively reduce distractions in order to ensure optimal focus and productivity. Distractions have perpetually existed, yet their pervasiveness has significantly heightened with the advent of the information age. In the current 21st century milieu, an abundance of avenues now exist to divert our attention and cause us to lose track of time. Whether that is accomplished via electronic communication channels such as emails, text messages, social media platforms including Facebook, Twitter, Snapchat, Instagram, and Tinder, telephonic conversations, or by means of interpersonal interactions. Each of these activities has the potential to significantly divert your attention from your main objectives, contingent upon the nature of your engagement with them. If an individual is engaged in a significant project, any of these distractions has the potential to disrupt their concentration, thereby inhibiting their workflow. The term "flow" refers to the state of being completely absorbed and effectively progressing towards completing a task. This implies that dedicating your full concentration to accomplishing a single task enables the flourishing of creativity and the production of exceptional work. When an interruption arises, even if it is brief, it can necessitate a recovery period of approximately 20 minutes in order to regain the previous level of focus and productivity. It is imperative that you approach your work and priorities with a sense of urgency, conducting yourself in a prompt manner even if you have ample time to complete the task. Emulating this approach is the key to accomplishing tasks effectively. It encompasses the practice of exerting personal agency over one's daily affairs, ensuring that the individual remains the master of their schedule rather than becoming subject to the whims of external demands. Despite initiating diligent efforts towards task completion, the presence of distractions will inevitably impede your progress. Please refrain from permitting this occurrence. Please disengage from Facebook, place your phone in silent mode, or ideally, keep it out of your immediate vicinity. Additionally, kindly inform any individuals who might interrupt you during the specific hours dedicated to your significant undertaking. Ensure proactive preparation for the more substantial tasks, communicate your intentions to colleagues, and witness a collective atmosphere of understanding and respect. If alternative sources of interruptions persist, it is advisable to enhance one's ability to concentrate on the current task, thereby minimizing distractions through heightened focus.

Another significant factor to refrain from is the act of procrastination. Procrastination essentially refers to the act of delaying crucial tasks with significant impact until a later point in time. Students, in particular, tend to display this tendency of time mismanagement. They engage in the behavior of delaying their work by prioritizing smaller and less demanding tasks, instead of directing their utmost attention to the completion of the significant task at hand. Alternatively, it is postponed by one hour as they engage in viewing an episode of their preferred television series or while they partake in watching a film. In the majority of instances, engaging in procrastination carries a significant likelihood of transforming crucial tasks into both urgent and important matters, leading to the unnecessary experience of stress. When you commence the task at a later stage, you tend to expedite it, as your imminent deadline looms and you find yourself in a state of urgency. Consequently, there is a production of work that exhibits inferior quality. If one consistently grapples with procrastination, it could be opportune to embrace strategies and practices to mitigate its effects. If you happen to be experiencing procrastination, a recommended course of action is to devote your undivided attention to a single high-impact task for a maximum period of 10 minutes. Simply perform this task and then cease. You may discover that this simple action generates a small measure of impetus, prompting you to engage in productive work for a duration of 20 minutes, 30 minutes, or potentially even an hour. Procrastination typically ensues when one perceives the task at hand as exorbitant, thereby inducing a sense of being inundated and potentially giving rise to anxiousness. Previously, I elaborated on the effective utilization of a to-do list. The concept of breaking down substantial tasks into smaller, more manageable components is also relevant in this context. If immediate action is not initiated, kindly consider breaking down the tasks into smaller components. This approach will facilitate a more comprehensive understanding of the necessary actions to accomplish the task. In numerous instances, this approach will mitigate feelings of unease and facilitate psychological rejuvenation in preparation for upcoming tasks, as you will be focused on sequentially accomplishing individual steps rather than tackling all five steps simultaneously.

Step 5: Get Organized

Lack of organization results in subpar time management as it necessitates wasteful expenditure of time in the pursuit of crucial resources or documents amidst a disarray of clutter. Observing a disorganized workstation may give rise to the perception of a high workload, potentially leading to the inclination to evade or procrastinate on tasks at hand.

Whilst it is undeniable that possessing goals, a time plan, a priority list, and a time schedule can be beneficial, it should be noted that the lack of organizational skills may impede the successful achievement of said goals. Through the act of systematically arranging your workspace (e. In a conducive environment, such as a well-appointed study room or a dedicated office space, you are able to carry out your tasks with optimal efficiency and focus, without succumbing to feelings of being overwhelmed.

Methods for Organizing and Streamlining Your Workspace

"To streamline your workspace, employ the subsequent approach:

Please locate three containers and designate each of them as 'retain, discard, and donate.' Within the 'retain' container, deposit the items that are essential for your upcoming endeavors and will be utilized accordingly. In the designated 'donation' container, kindly deposit any possessions that are superfluous to your requirements but have potential for sale, charitable contribution, or presenting as gifts to acquaintances or family members. Lastly, within the designated "discard" container, arrange the assortment of remaining items that are neither required nor of any utility to any individual, and generously distribute these; such items may encompass shattered kitchenware, tattered volumes of literature, and the like. Discard these items immediately.

What course of action would you suggest taking from here? We shall address this matter in the subsequent chapter.

Step 6: Strategize Your Time

Create a comprehensive schedule outlining each and every second, minute, and hour of your daily agenda. The process of organizing your time will be influenced by your personal work preferences, whether you are more productive in the morning, afternoon, or evening, and the surroundings in which you find it most conducive to complete your tasks. In order to effectively organize your day, it is necessary to engage in prior planning of your various activities or tasks.

There are several crucial factors that should be taken into account when engaging in preliminary planning of your activities or tasks:

Prearrange Your Day in Advance: Prior to retiring for the night, ensure that you have meticulously organized your forthcoming day's engagements and duties. Please record your activities in order of priority, assigning appropriate time slots to each activity, and ensure you have adequately prepared all necessary resources for the completion of each task and activity.

If you tend to invest significant time in the process of selecting your attire, I would suggest arranging your clothing prior to retiring for the night. By employing this technique, you will effectively eliminate the need to expend time and energy in the morning deliberating on which activities to engage in, or on matters such as wardrobe choices.

Do Not Feel Overburdened: Irrespective of the length of your task list or the apparent busyness of your forthcoming day, it is imperative that you do not succumb to a sense of being overwhelmed. Instead, devise a comprehensive plan for your day encompassing the effective execution of each task, allocating specific time slots for each activity, and keeping in mind the significance and potential rewards that result from accomplishing each item on your agenda. Ultimately, by the conclusion of each day or week, you will have successfully achieved your predetermined objectives devoid of lamenting the extent of your workload.

Rise and Shine at the Crack of Dawn: Initiate your day promptly by awakening early; while it may pose a challenge, make an earnest attempt to do so. Establish an alarm and ensure its activation on a nightly basis. Rising at an early hour will afford you ample time to adequately prepare yourself both mentally and physically.

By rising early, one's mental preparedness for the day's engagements enhances, allowing sufficient time to accomplish one's morning rituals prior to commencing planned duties or activities. The state of confusion arising from the morning rush will engender a bewildering and anxiety-inducing day ahead. Moreover, in the event that you were unable to allocate sufficient time beforehand to arrange your schedule and tasks, rising early in the morning affords you the opportunity to accomplish these objectives.

Adopting an early sleep schedule often necessitates making certain concessions, such as forsaking indulgence in one's beloved television program, abstaining from late-night internet usage, or refraining from nocturnal conversations with friends. In order to ensure the successful implementation of the time management process, it is imperative to make these requisite sacrifices. What measures can one take to rise early in the morning despite having slept late? This is a feasible possibility, however, it is likely that you will experience fatigue throughout the course of the day.

It is necessary for one to allow their body and mind to unwind and make necessary preparations for the forthcoming engagements of the following day. By adequately resting your body, you will enhance your ability to focus on your activities and reduce the likelihood of experiencing daytime drowsiness.

Record the Perturbing Activity or Task: There is consistently that singular matter that has been causing discomfort or concern for an extended period. Make sure to document it daily while you are in the process of devising your plan, even if you lack a solution or are uncertain about the approach. Do not omit this step until it is completed, regardless of the circumstances.

It is highly improbable that you would continue to document your troubling activities or responsibilities for an extended period of time, without taking any action or finding a viable solution to address them. Whenever you revisit your plan, it will serve as a constant reminder prompting you to conduct thorough research and ultimately address the matter at hand.

In the subsequent phase, we will acquire the knowledge and skills necessary to arrange your time in a manner that ensures the efficient management of your time.

Alter Your Perspective On Time And Your Approach To Work.

There are multiple strategies available for optimizing your work approach to enhance productivity and accomplish tasks more efficiently. You may already be engaging in some of these activities, while others may be unfamiliar to you. These tips can be utilized individually or in combination with one another, and have the potential to significantly enhance your productivity levels.

Time is a concept that can be perceived in two significant ways - as a valuable commodity, akin to money, and as a gateway to possibilities and chances that should not be squandered. Assign a monetary worth to your time. Consider the monetary value assigned to each hour of your time. This will aid in the assessment of optimal time allocation, as well as the identification of tasks suitable for delegation. It may be alluring to engage in numerous tasks single-handedly, especially if one believes they can accomplish them more expediently or to a higher standard. However, such an approach proves to be time-consuming in the grand scheme of things. Allocate resources towards delegation and the accompanying assistance at an early stage, which will aid in the development and motivation of a team that will ultimately result in time and energy savings in the long run. Furthermore, when one conceives of time as a valuable opportunity, there arises a desire to utilize it with utmost efficacy, consequently compelling a transformation in one's approach to work.

Give priority: The crucial aspect of efficient time management lies in allocating priority to tasks of significant value. To achieve this, it is imperative to possess a clear understanding of your objectives and the means by which you can effectively pursue them. Please clarify your objectives, tactics, and the necessary steps that must be taken to accomplish them. Please execute this action for both immediate and extended durations. Upon identifying your true objectives (and the underlying motivations behind them), it becomes simpler to make informed choices regarding the necessary steps and their prioritization, enabling you to effectively devise a corresponding plan. It is imperative to prioritize focusing on the fundamentals initially as this will establish a solid groundwork for your objectives, subsequently leading to the achievement of the remaining tasks. Once you have compiled your roster of objectives and the corresponding measures, you can proceed to establishing timelines for the completion of each item, arranging them in order of significance, formulating a strategic blueprint for attaining each goal within its designated timeframe, and subsequently progressing through your agenda.

Prioritize vital tasks: Refrain from convincing yourself that you are not inclined to be productive in the morning or that you function better during the night, and consequently using this as an excuse to delay crucial or challenging responsibilities until later in the day. Direct your attention towards your highest priorities and commence your efforts on tasks that demand greater concentration and vitality during the earlier parts of the day. If it holds significance, your foremost objective should be to accomplish it. Rest assured, you will experience a profound sense of accomplishment, and you will find the remaining tasks significantly easier to complete, as if they were effortless. Moreover, it is highly probable that you will proceed through them with greater speed and minimal difficulty.

Establish attainable time parameters: I must confess that I have tended to excessively impose deadlines upon myself in order to accomplish a substantial amount of work swiftly, thereby neglecting to allocate an appropriate length of time for task completion. I would invariably find myself attempting to manage all tasks independently, extending my working hours beyond what is advisable, solely to fulfill self-imposed time constraints. As a consequence, my ability to concentrate waned as I found myself expending my energy on the self-imposed pressure arising from these deadlines. Avoid repeating the same error; adhere to practical timeframes, and if you discover that tasks can be completed ahead of schedule, seize the opportunity. This approach will enhance your motivation and foster a more positive mindset, as opposed to being burdened with the task of catching up after falling behind due to impractical deadlines. Apportioning time to tasks also alleviates superfluous distress stemming from the awareness of numerous impending tasks, without certainty regarding the adequacy of time to fulfill each within their respective deadlines.

Mitigate factors that consume time: Identify all activities that result in unproductive time expenditure without contributing value, and proactively restrict or eliminate them. This may manifest as individuals and/or endeavors. Please be reminded that by removing activities that are unproductive, you can create additional time that can be devoted to more meaningful pursuits. This can enhance the quality of relationships, mitigate stress levels, and contribute to the attainment of goals. A significant drain on productivity that often goes unnoticed is the allocation of time towards reviewing and purging emails originating from subscriptions of which one may be unaware. Please allocate some time to unsubscribe from these, as doing so will ultimately result in significant time savings in the future and enable you to prioritize what truly matters. Another source of inefficiency arises from unproductive meetings. If you are tasked with organizing a meeting, it is imperative that you ascertain that the objective is unambiguous, that a well-defined agenda is in place, and that all participants are directed to adhere to the subject matter. Ensure the establishment of unambiguous objectives and eradicate superfluous meetings. Consistently contemplate the objective and the intended as well as potential consequences of your actions. Consider the extent to which your activities contribute to the completion of tasks, or assess whether you are purposefully avoiding productive behavior. Please provide an accurate response. Reflect upon the wisdom espoused by Peter Drucker, who proclaimed, "The epitome of futility lies in executing with great efficiency tasks that bear no significance." Engage in thorough introspection of your endeavors and undoubtedly you shall ascertain several unproductive endeavors that can be expunged or modified, thereby allowing you to optimize your allocation of time towards the attainment of worthwhile objectives with utmost efficiency.

Allocate time for email management: Unless the completion of your tasks is significantly dependent on the outcomes of email communications, the constant influx of emails throughout the day has the potential to divert your attention from prioritized tasks. I acknowledge that in the current era of advanced technology and widespread information access, there is a prevailing expectation for prompt responses and constant availability. However, similar to how you would prioritize other responsibilities, it is advisable to implement a strategic approach to managing email communication. If there are emails of utmost importance that you anticipate receiving, it is advisable to periodically review your email inbox, such as every thirty minutes, and allocate your work hours accordingly. Restrict your email responses to urgent matters exclusively during that period, and designate determined time slots throughout the day to address other non-urgent emails, such as prior to lunch and towards the close of business hours. Remove unproductive interactions and consistently redirect your attention towards matters of high importance. Employ the identical principle to as numerous tasks as feasible.

Establish a designated work and rest schedule: While it is often recommended to engage in 90-minute work sessions with 10-minute intervals for breaks, it is imperative to ascertain the most suitable work cycles for your own needs. As a guideline, adopting shorter work intervals of approximately one to two hours, punctuated by periodic breaks, can aid in maintaining concentration.

Exercise discretion in your availability: It is advisable not to make yourself constantly accessible to everyone. Yielding to anyone seeking your attention at any given time can potentially divert your focus from more consequential tasks. Acquire the ability to decline requests and consistently verify your schedule before making any new commitments. Establish the duration and designated periods during which you will commit to engaging with your colleagues for work-related matters and ensure that individuals are duly informed in this regard. Allocate time for family, friends, and individuals of significance, while minimizing work-related interruptions to this schedule unless absolutely essential. This will not only facilitate effective time management and organization, but will also contribute to enhanced work-life equilibrium. Do not let others steer you away from your primary goals.

Technological assistance: A plethora of user-friendly and highly beneficial time management applications are readily available at no cost. These tools can assist you in effectively arranging and assigning priority to tasks, identifying and preventing scheduling conflicts, pinpointing instances where an excessive number of tasks are designated for a single day, as well as indicating areas where time is potentially being excessively allocated or inefficiently utilized. Furthermore, employ technology and applications to establish robust systems that encompass functions such as record-keeping, information management, communication facilitation, and surveillance. These facilitate efficient task management, enhancing productivity, and affording ample leisure time for pursuing other activities according to personal preference.

Engage in activities that bring you pleasure: You will experience enhanced motivation when you dedicate more time to activities that bring you joy. I comprehend that circumstances may occasionally render this unfeasible, but whenever viable, incorporate a pleasurable activity into your timetable and roster of obligations. This will result in increased motivation and vitality, and tasks that are less pleasurable become more manageable when anticipation for something better exists. While it may appear as if you are excessively controlling your life, by incorporating personal activities into your schedule, you guarantee that you are dedicating time to your family, friends, health, and enjoyable pursuits as well. As a result, there is an enhancement in the equilibrium between work and personal life, a reduction in stress levels, a heightened concentration, and a rise in energy levels.

Review and Repeat: Evaluate your daily achievements and make necessary adjustments to identify tasks for the next day, including those requiring continuation or rescheduling. Do not conclude the day burdened by a mind occupied with matters that require reorganization. If there is a need to make adjustments to the timelines and reschedule tasks, please proceed accordingly. Additionally, consider pondering upon strategies and techniques that you have employed successfully, and if they are replicable, subsequently incorporate them within your overall strategy for subsequent endeavors, whilst determining the components that integrate seamlessly into a standardized routine. In addition, it is important to consider evaluating whether the actions being implemented are effectively achieving their intended goals, or if it is necessary to revise them accordingly. Do not undertake actions solely on the basis of their inclusion in the plan, as this may lead to significant time wastage. Hindsight leads to foresight. Execute actions that prove efficacious in leading you towards your desired outcome. Please bear in mind that this plan is entirely yours, providing you with the flexibility to modify it as you see fit.

Time Management Techniques

In the context of commerce, time is universally acknowledged as a valuable and fungible resource. Hence, it is crucial to optimize your daily schedule to enhance your overall daily productivity. Frequently, the task of effectively managing time can prove challenging, particularly in situations where there is an abundance of tasks to be completed and only a limited number of hours in which to accomplish them. Nevertheless, there are measures that can be implemented to maximize productivity during stressful, time-constrained days, enabling you to utilize every minute to its full potential. It is remarkably effortless to encounter time wastage, often transpiring inadvertently.

Engaging in activities outside of your daily routine, detracts from dedicating time to crucial tasks that demand your attention. Hence, it is imperative for individuals to acquire proficiency in time management techniques in order to minimize time wastage. Outlined below are several critical strategies that you should commence implementing immediately:

Always work with lists

The utilization of lists is a widely employed and highly efficient strategy in the realm of time management. It is necessary for you to generate lists that facilitate your daily tasks. The following lists could be taken into consideration:

The daily itinerary - this encompasses all the tasks and activities that must be completed within a day. It is imperative to establish a daily routine in order to facilitate the seamless progression and completion of work and tasks throughout your life.

Task list- This is a compilation of obligations and responsibilities to be accomplished within a designated time frame, encompassing monthly, weekly, and daily activities. The list should consist of tasks that have been arranged in ascending order of priority based on their significance.

A roster of individuals to contact- this compilation holds particular significance, as it encompasses the identities and contact details of individuals you must reach out to within a given day. This guarantees that you are contacting at the appropriate moment and that you are not inadvertently overlooking any crucial calls. Once more, it is imperative that you assign priority rankings to the individuals listed, placing the utmost importance on reaching out to the primary contact and gradually diminishing the significance of subsequent calls.

A conference organizer ought to possess a comprehensive set of instructions outlining the procedures and protocols to be followed during a conference or meeting. This ensures that no crucial matters are inadvertently omitted, thereby mitigating the need for a subsequent meeting to address any overlooked items.

In contemporary times, there exist sophisticated systems that facilitate the creation of significant records, thereby enabling individuals to efficiently oversee their time.

Attend fewer meetings

If you have not yet discerned, meetings are not particularly productive. To enhance productivity and optimize time utilization, it is advisable to minimize the frequency of meetings. Many individuals utilize meetings as a means to escape from their daily tasks. Nevertheless, for individuals seeking to assess their daily achievements, meetings prove to be of limited utility. In order to accomplish your tasks efficiently, it is imperative that you formulate a strategic plan to minimize the frequency of meetings. If you are presiding over a meeting, it implies that your presence is required. It is imperative for you to devise an effective plan that will facilitate your ability to prioritize crucial matters. Subsequently, you can succinctly outline the key points discussed during the meeting, enabling you to seamlessly proceed with your tasks. If attendance at a meeting is obligatory, it is necessary to employ strategies to respectfully prioritize your time when the meeting begins to consume excessive amounts of it.

Block your time table

The key to achieving minimal unassigned time is through the implementation of this strategy. By doing so, you will have ample time to complete the tasks that are outlined in your schedule. In the event that you exclude idle time from your schedule, there is a higher likelihood that you will be inclined to allocate that time towards activities that are not advantageous or prioritize less important matters, despite having a significant workload to accomplish within the day. Allocate dedicated time for high-priority tasks as well, in order to safeguard against any disruptions in your schedule during the execution of these responsibilities. It is advisable to proactively block your calendar well in advance, even prior to determining the specific activities for the day, in order to prevent the allocation of crucial time to tasks of lesser importance. It is important to recognize that at that point, you will have a significant amount of free time available to allocate towards important tasks.

Utilize your surplus leisure time effectively

There are ample possibilities to maximize productivity and prioritize more essential tasks during the short intervals or extended durations one devotes to relatively insignificant activities. For example, when one is traveling, a considerable amount of time is often futilely spent during the process of waiting to board an aircraft. During that period, there exist significant literary works that you can peruse, which can greatly contribute to enhancing the quality of your professional endeavors. You may also choose to view inspirational videos. This presents an opportune moment for making callbacks and responding to emails, as well as dispatching crucial communications to clients. This can also be an important time to strategize on what needs to be donein order to better your work and productivity. Additionally, this period can provide an opportunity for reflection on the accomplishments you have attained thus far, as well as the development of effective strategies to enhance your work performance. Consider the multitude of minutes that are squandered throughout the course of a day, which could otherwise be utilized productively.

Time managementrequires discipline. While others are engaged in leisurely pursuits, it is prudent for you to contemplate the substantial accomplishments that can be attained by investing time wisely. Although it may appear inconsequential, squandering ten minutes within your tightly structured agenda can accumulate to a significant loss of time over the course of a day or even a week.

Maintaining One's Motivation Amidst Unfavorable Circumstances

Motivation can significantly influence the extent of your success in crafting and diligently pursuing your objectives. Individuals frequently discover that once they have attained the bare minimum in their daily pursuits, the impetus wanes, resulting in the abandonment of their goals without further consideration. If you consistently prioritize procrastination due to a lack of motivation, you are effectively impeding your own progress and hindering opportunities for personal growth and achievement. If you happen to belong to this group of individuals, it is imperative that you explore avenues that can serve as incentives driving you towards achieving success.

Which strategies have proven effective in maintaining your motivation in previous instances? In what manner can you leverage the strategies employed previously to support your present objectives? By identifying the factors that have contributed to your past achievements in the realm of goal setting, you can discover alternative methods to sustain your motivation, even during moments when the desired outcome appears elusive. Let us now examine various strategies that can help you maintain motivation amidst challenging circumstances.

Compose inspirational messages for yourself that will serve as a source of strength during moments of despair.

When I find myself in need of motivation during my day, I shall proceed to place arbitrary adhesive notes in various locations within my residence and workspace. Although some may perceive it as unconventional, the small cues and motivational notes provided by these paper artifacts enable me to persistently pursue my objective. Consider producing a handful of these items and strategically placing them in accessible locations that will facilitate your progress towards achieving your objectives.

Engage the assistance of a companion to motivate and propel you towards greater achievements.

Similar to the presence of an accountability partner, consider the value of having an individual who will actively encourage and propel you forward. It is not necessary to engage in a persistent or nagging form of urging. They have the capacity to inquire about your whereabouts and motivate you to proceed to the subsequent stage. This can be particularly advantageous in the event that you are experiencing emotional distress and considering relinquishing the entirety of your objective. We have all experienced similar situations, and having an individual who is eager to motivate us will assist us in maximizing our potential within the existing conditions and moving ahead.

Utilize Strategies to Maintain a Strong Focus on the Ultimate Objective

Maintaining a steadfast focus on the ultimate outcome of your objective can serve as an effective strategy to sustain motivation and perseverance throughout your daily pursuits. Take, for instance, the objective of weight reduction. Nevertheless, the circumstances of today have proven to be immensely challenging, and the presence of an irresistible slice of cake residing in the refrigerator exacerbates the situation. Please pause for a moment and envisage the transformative outcome when you successfully shed the weight that you desire to shed. The aforementioned thought and objective can assist you in exercising restraint, thereby avoiding actions that may hinder your attainment of the ultimate objective.

Integrate Your Objectives within Your Timetable

If you encounter a lack of sufficient time to complete your desired tasks, make an effort to integrate those actions into your regular schedule. One can achieve the objective by appearing to exert minimal effort, and by strategically incorporating certain activities into one's schedule, it becomes possible to effectively progress towards the desired outcome without significant additional exertion. Discover strategies to organically integrate the components necessary for achieving the objective and consistently engage in their execution throughout your day to acquire the requisite expertise or fundamental elements imperative for advancing towards your goal.

Do not let setbacks deter you from progressing further.

Existence has the potential to be immensely disheartening. Let's face it. There will be instances wherein the attainment of your objective may appear futile. You may feel compelled to relinquish, as persevering through the challenges encountered on the path towards your objective may appear to be the most convenient option. Nevertheless, it is imperative that you transcend these obstacles and continue to progress. Unfortunately, you were not successful in obtaining the promotion you had aspired for. Rather than allowing oneself to wallow in feelings of envy and resentment, endeavor to seize the forthcoming opportunity. There is an area for improvement that you can focus on to enhance your readiness for the upcoming round of promotions. The non-occurrence of an event according to your desired schedule does not imply its permanent impossibility. It implies that it is intended for a different occasion.

Mastering the Art of Overcoming Hurdles

Difficulties will pose a significant challenge to your ability to sustain motivation. When confronted by obstacles, individuals may find it more convenient to relinquish their objectives and abandon them, as opposed to confronting the challenges head-on and persisting towards their achievement. You will not attain your objectives unless you acquire the ability to persistently overcome the impediments that hinder your progress. Regardless of the seemingly bleak circumstances, there is always a viable avenue to manifest your aspirations and ambitions.

Please bear this in mind for future reference when faced with future obstacles.

Maintaining one's motivation can prove challenging at times. When one is engaged in a hectic lifestyle, it can be convenient to defer one's goals upon encountering difficulties in their pursuit. You have numerous commitments and opportunities at hand, making it more convenient to relinquish your goals rather than persisting and settling for your current circumstances. Do not allow yourself to become subject to the conditions surrounding you. Overcome the challenges and cultivate a formidable presence. The greater capacity you develop to sustain self-motivation and surmount obstacles, the more proficient you will grow in achieving your objectives.

Commencing Your Work:

A man who consistently delays his decision-making will ultimately find that circumstances dictate his choices. Thompson

In the aforementioned profound statement, Mr. Thompson eloquently delineates the repercussions of succumbing to the tendency to postpone tasks. When one consistently protracts the completion of their tasks, ultimately, there arises a necessity to respond in accordance with prevailing circumstances.

Failure to submit a critical project in a timely manner, resulting in the loss of a significant client for your company, could potentially lead to termination of your employment, which would be justified under the circumstances. In the event that such a situation arises, you would be left with no alternative but to conform to the directive of the company, as any course of action at that point would be deemed untimely.

Monstrous procrastination exemplifies the allure of postponing tasks initially, yet it is solely when one must endure the repercussions that the error becomes apparent. In order to protect oneself from such situations, it is advisable to promptly commence with the execution of daily action plans and To-do lists.

"Presented below are effective strategies and techniques that can enable you to overcome procrastination and substantially enhance your productivity:

The Quick Solution

With an impressive track record of delivering remarkable results for numerous individuals, the 2-minute hack unquestionably holds the potential to yield positive outcomes for you as well. This effective technique possesses the capability to halt procrastination by cleverly inducing your mind into committing to tasks.

When you have reached the state of preparedness for engaging in a particular task, particularly if the task at hand poses considerable difficulty, simply affirm to yourself that you will dedicate a mere 2 minutes to its completion, adhering strictly to this time constraint. Examine the advantages associated with undertaking the aforementioned task, as well as the broader perspective: the gratification you will derive from completing the chore can serve as a driving force for your motivation. Once you are prepared to initiate the task, kindly set a timer for a duration of 2 minutes, and commence the execution of the given assignment.

It is highly probable that shortly after commencing the task, you will experience a sense of engagement and continue working on it even after the designated timer expires. In the event that you lack enthusiasm for the task, even after the timer commences its auditory indication, mentally prompt yourself to engage in another consecutive interval of two minutes and subsequently reset the timer. Continue executing this process until approximately 20 to 30 percent of the task has been accomplished. Once you have reached that juncture, you will be astounded by the level of productivity attained, undoubtedly compelling you to continue onwards.

Strictly adhere to predetermined time limits for each of your tasks.

An effective method of overcoming procrastination and enhancing productivity is to allocate specific time slots for your tasks. The concept of time boxing entails the imposition of specific time constraints on a given activity. As an example, one might allocate a predetermined duration for conducting research in pursuit of a new novel, thereby confining the activity within the confines of this temporal limitation.

If you intend to dedicate two hours to selecting a suitable research topic, it is advisable to discontinue your efforts once the allocated time period has concluded. This guarantees that you do not indefinitely devote your efforts to a single task, nor do you unwisely postpone all the remaining obligations that eagerly demand your attention.

Decline Requests and Distractions

Frequently, the disturbances in your vicinity serve as catalysts for indulging in procrastination. Specifically, prioritizing the needs of others before attending to your own and willingly accommodating interruptions are two major contributing factors to the prevalent habit of procrastination among individuals.

As an example, consider the situation in which you have made all necessary preparations to commence work, when suddenly a close acquaintance arrives and beseeches your aid in carrying out their crucial undertaking. Instead of telling that friend that you are busy with your work, you happily give in and help that friend. This diverts your attention from your designated assignment.

In order to cultivate proficiency in time management, it is imperative to address the following matter: the necessity to abstain from distractions. Learning to exercise assertiveness by declining requests from others, as well as resisting one's own impulses, is crucial to avoid constant disruptions while attempting to focus on tasks at hand. In order to accomplish this, initially consider all potential disturbances and factors that could divert your attention from the task at hand, and compile a comprehensive inventory.

Furthermore, consider devising strategies to decline such interruptions and maintain concentration on your tasks. If an acquaintance consistently contacts you during your work commitments, kindly inform them that you are engaged in an important task and will reach out to them at a more suitable time. If the aforementioned acquaintance persists in troubling you, we advise that you power down your cellular device.

If you find yourself inclined to view movies on Netflix whenever you access your laptop for the purpose of conducting research for your book, it is advisable to employ measures that restrict access to the website for a designated period of time. Utilizing tools such as LeechBlock (a Mozilla Firefox add-on), StayFocusd (a Google Chrome Extension), or similar applications will help maintain focus and avoid unnecessary distractions. Experiment with various strategies for addressing distractions, and you will gradually regain control over your impulses and the pressures exerted by external factors.

Indulge in a Well-Deserved Incentive

One advisable approach to motivate oneself to complete a specific task is to entice through the provision of an incentive. Select a pleasant reward that you may find enjoyable upon the successful completion of a task, and subsequently indulge yourself with it. Upon completing the composition of your upcoming eBook, which you intend to present to your esteemed subscribers, you may consider indulging in your preferred burger at the esteemed establishment of your choice. Alternatively, after engaging in an hour-long exercise regimen, you and your significant other may opt to embark on a romantic outing together.

Rewards serve as a means of positive reinforcement, effectively encouraging the development of good routines and practices, thereby facilitating their transformation into ingrained habits. Hence, grant yourself a reward each time you faithfully adhere to the time management techniques expounded in this book, and you shall instill them as habitual practices.

With that being acknowledged, the opposite also holds true. What consequences can be expected for the unsuccessful completion of a task? The absence of a date, the withholding of a candy bar, or, in a more severe scenario, being sent to one's room without dinner! Negative reinforcement can be equally as influential as positive reinforcement.

To significantly enhance your productivity, it is crucial to maintain unwavering focus on your tasks. What is the method by which you can accomplish that? The subsequent chapter will delve into precisely that topic.

Reward Yourself

It is my hope that you followed my suggestion and proceeded to generate a comprehensive list of tasks to be accomplished. Now let us return to the line of reasoning.

The concept of reward is unparalleled in its positive attributes. I shall not dispute this reality, as it is universally acknowledged that individuals harbor an inherent affinity for incentives, be they considerable or even trivial in nature. A recommended course of action would be to maintain a diary or a planner. The utilization of pen and paper in the realm of life management is quite extensive, as you may have observed. It has the potential to cultivate discipline within oneself. There are certainly available peripherals that render the conventional use of pen and paper unnecessary, and if you possess an affinity for technology, it serves as an excellent means of utilizing it. If one holds traditional values and favors conventional methods, there is no inherent detriment in doing so. Scholars have determined that, at present, no viable replacement exists for the act of manual writing.

Within your personal organizer, create a timetable outlining your daily tasks and engagements. Please feel free to include specific details, such as the precise hour. Compensate yourself for every accomplished task. Within the rewards, you may choose to grant access to one of your social accounts, indulge in television viewing, engage in reading a book, partake in restorative nap, relish in consuming your preferred snack, or enjoy playing your favorite game. It is imperative to ensure the inclusion of these rewards within the designated schedule. Maintain integrity in self-reflection and ensure adherence to the prescribed timetable. You may find it astonishing to observe the extent to which your own personal development is evident when confronted with an incomplete task.

The primary objective of indulging in self-rewards is to cultivate and enhance self-discipline. With dedication and substantial exertion, one can utilize positive reinforcement to achieve enhanced productivity, albeit requiring a significant investment of time. There is a supplementary approach - negative reinforcement, although it is advisable to exercise moderation in self-criticism.

There is no inherent detriment in committing errors; in fact, repeated blunders may not pose any harm as long as they do not involve external entities. However, it is essential to establish an explicit boundary that signifies when one ought to cease and rectify their missteps.

In regard to the reward benefit system, it is imperative to guarantee that the rewards align with your work regimen. It is inconsequential to maintain a reward system that undermines the diligent efforts being exerted. Exhibit generosity but exercise prudence.

Allow me to elucidate this concept by providing a concise illustration.

Let us consider the scenario where you are actively engaged in the pursuit of weight reduction. You have exerted considerable effort and have successfully achieved the desired weight you desired for yourself. This noteworthy accomplishment certainly warrants commendation. Would it be appropriate to indulge in an unlimited buffet as a means of rewarding oneself?

No, succinctly stated, it will not prove advantageous to either of you in the immediate or the extended duration.

You are not only endangering yourself by yielding to temptation, but you are also establishing a detrimental precedent for your future self. A more prudent incentive could entail receiving a modest-sized pizza or a similarly light alternative. It is crucial that it holds allure and appeal for you, while the compensation must also align systematically with your individual universe.

These matters may appear daunting initially. Certain individuals may perceive the situation as being both intimidating and challenging. It is imperative to comprehend that individuals typically experience apprehension towards the unfamiliar or untested aspects of their lives. It comprises a blend of trust in the unknown, driving force, and the eagerness to develop in order to surmount the customary apprehension associated with taking the initial step. After completing the initial phase, proceed without interruption, even upon encountering subsequent obstacles.

Pausing halfway through is considerably preferable to resting before initiating any tasks.

Spending Free Time Passionately

Having successfully utilized the Time Optimization System to effectively allocate your time, it is now opportune to employ the fruits of your labor in a valuable manner.

It has been expressed that the invaluable nature of time persists and continues to be one of the most limited resources in human existence.

An idea can only be implemented if it is solidified by being recorded in a dedicated schedule, and all tasks outlined in the schedule must be completed in order to effectively manage one's time. This encompasses the manner in which you allocate your leisure hours. Failure to dedicate your leisure time to personal growth and engaging in activities that bring you genuine joy and satisfaction will impede your ability to find the motivation necessary to lead a rich and successful existence. Leisure time ought to be dedicated to the formation of delightful memories and gratifying experiences. Given the limited time we have in this world, it is imperative that we dedicate our days to pursuing activities that bring us joy.

You dedicate a significant portion of your life to work, and the limited leisure time you receive is the utmost gratification one can enjoy. While it is true that individuals must engage in labor to sustain themselves, the allocation of one's leisure time remains a matter of personal discretion.

The primary focus of Taking Control of Time predominantly lies in the pursuit of time liberation, though it is of utmost importance to allocate the freed-up time towards engaging in activities that bring one joy and fulfillment.

Life is ephemeral and can be allocated in two divergent manners.

Living passionately

Spending time.

Engaging in professional duties occupies one's time during work hours, while the remainder of one's life can be dedicated to pursuing one's passions with enthusiasm. By effectively improving your hourly wage in the workplace, you create opportunities to enhance your experiences through additional thrilling endeavors, since you will be able to achieve a salary increase while reducing your working hours.

However, the true challenge commences upon the moment of free availability. Irrespective of one's desire to acquire proficiency in a musical instrument, engage in travel and exploration, pursue knowledge, or simply indulge in leisurely activities such as watching television, consuming news, or participating in games, existence presents itself as a playground. The Second Principle of Time emphasizes the importance of utilizing one's leisure time to engage in activities that bring joy and fulfillment. Failure to pursue your aspirations and interests in life will inevitably lead to a lack of productivity in the workplace, resulting in a propensity to be idle during working hours, ultimately undermining the fundamental tenet of effective time management.

PROCEDURES FOR IMPLEMENTING THE SECOND TIME PRINCIPLE:

Examine your passions and consider what activities bring you joy. Engage in regular weekly brainstorming sessions lasting between 15 minutes to 1 hour, with the objective of formulating optimal strategies for effectively utilizing your time. Additionally, allocate a portion of your schedule to envisioning a hypothetical scenario in which you experienced a day without any financial or personal limitations. This will enable your mind to achieve a state of liberation and facilitate your understanding of the underlying motivators that guide you throughout the course of your work week. Identify opportunities within your work schedule where you can allocate time for personal pursuits. If one derives pleasure from engaging in bowling, hiking, socializing with acquaintances, or strumming melodies on a guitar. Feel free to allocate your leisure time as you please and incorporate it into your schedule.

Planning

There are several benefits to engaging in the strategic allocation of your energy. Initially, it alleviates the stress that arises from the demands of your professional and personal commitments. One is aware of the tasks they will undertake throughout the day, and each item that is checked off from their daily itinerary bestows upon them a sense of fulfillment. The cumulative effect of establishing a schedule and adhering to it is that you are more likely to successfully attain your goals and objectives.

The key to formulating an effective plan lies in articulating goals that are not only highly relevant, but also measurable, thereby enabling a comprehensive assessment of your progress. A strategic approach known as the S.M.A.R.T strategy has been developed to address long-standing objectives that require definition. Currently, there exists a specific approach to refine it into the S.M.A.R.T.E.R framework. Shall we examine how this technique operates within the context of the organizational process?

The systematic approach to planning using the S.M.A.R.T.E.R technique

The letter S stands for explicit, calling for the clear delineation of objectives rather than being vague or comprehensive. The symbol 'M' denotes measurability and signifies the need to define specific criteria by which to assess your progress. The A method achievable. This methodology does not encourage you to surpass your limitations. Given equal circumstances, the focus lies in prudently delineating those boundaries. The inclusion of the R symbol bears great significance as it strongly suggests the importance of diligently verifying whether the objective aligns with your vision of enhancing your skills as a time manager. The letter T symbolizes the concept of time, therefore it is imperative to evaluate the timeframe within which you intend to accomplish your objectives.

The additional letters E and R symbolize the acts of evaluating and once more altering, individually. These correspondences exemplify the importance of consistently evaluating your objectives and performance, in order to determine the direction in which you are headed and make necessary adjustments.

Creating to-do lists

In terms of efficiently managing time or any form of organization, it is important to always bear in mind the proverb that states, "Even the least capable tool is more valuable than the sharpest intellect."

A daily agenda serves as a respectable visual representation of the tasks that need to be accomplished. It is also highly versatile in nature - it can be affixed to your computer monitor, accessed within your computer's software, installed as a mobile application, or transcribed onto a notebook.

Arrange it within the vicinity of your workspace. We should examine the steps involved in establishing your To-Do List.

The first step entails recording all of the tasks you need to complete. You have the option to either consolidate all your work and individual endeavors within a singular location or establish distinct records for each. Similarly, in the event that a substantial task arises, one can partition it into smaller components.

After documenting the tasks, the next step will involve establishing a prioritization framework for them. I have already analyzed the various methods through which one can prioritize tasks. Employ one of these methodologies or devise an alternative approach. Once you have completed attending to your errands, please consult your agenda to verify that all items are properly categorized. Once you are satisfied with your itinerary, proceed to enhance the tasks according to their respective priorities. Engaging in the utilization of task management applications

While generating a physical To-Do list can be effortless and portable, employing an application proves advantageous due to its incorporation of supplementary functionalities such as timely reminders, expediting task organization, and seamless sharing of the list with collaborators.

There exist a plethora of task management applications suitable for organizing tasks, such as TickTick, Things, and Todoist. We should examine the features of one of these: TickTick. The application enables users to assemble tasks with deadlines, attachments, and markers, and automatically generate assignments through the integration with Zaiper from Slack and Gmail messages. The application also provides the capability to conveniently consolidate your appointments in one centralized location, as it seamlessly integrates with select third-party calendars. Additionally, it offers the flexibility to incorporate subtasks as desired.

One unique feature that sets it apart from other competitors is the integrated Pomodoro timer. The Pomodoro technique is a distinguished approach to time management, wherein one dedicates their complete attention to a task for a duration of 25 minutes, followed by a brief intermission.

Operating within designated time intervals

Time allocation is a process whereby you designate a specific duration for a particular task. Therefore, it is commonly referred to as monotasking. One must consider the incorporation of time blocking as a strategy due to its ability to enhance focus and concentration. Instead of allowing yourself to handle multiple tasks, you are dedicating your attention to a single objective over an extended duration. From this perspective, the interference of time contradicts what many of us recall as the appropriate course of action.

Although multitasking may be effective for certain individuals, the prevalent reality for a significant number of people is that engaging in dual activities simultaneously is not a favorable strategy, as it results in the dispersion of one's focus. Research also indicates that there is often a discrepancy in accurately assessing our ability to multitask. The study also indicated that individuals who frequently engage in multitasking do so because they possess a reduced ability to ignore distractions and concentrate solely on one task. Devoting exclusive attention to one task at a time offers several benefits, yet before constructing a schedule based on time blocks, it is imperative to also bear in mind some of the limitations associated with this approach.

The primary examination lies in your genuine commitment to allocate sufficient time to meticulously plan out the utilization of each hour within your day. Similarly, it is imperative that you exercise prudence when determining the duration of a task and incorporate some flexibility to account for inevitable disruptions in the schedule. If you have a recurring schedule that requires frequent adjustments, implementing time blocking may present certain challenges.

do make due. You devote efforts to establishing one schedule, only to subsequently adapt it in response to a different request or requirement.

The crucial aspect of time blocking is to organize your agenda in a manner that allows for dedicated time slots to address your responsive tasks, such as responding to messages and emails, participating in meetings, and so forth. However, employ the strategy of time blocking in such a manner that none of these tasks impede your workflow. For instance, you may commence the day with a sixty-minute session devoted to tasks pertaining to your occupation, succeeded by a thirty-minute period allocated for the purpose of reviewing and responding to electronic correspondence and messages. Subsequently, allocate an additional half hour to deliver the children to their educational institution following this scheduled interval.

Avoiding Procrastination

Have you ever encountered a situation similar to this: where you are presented with a crucial task, yet find yourself engaged in various distractions, causing the prioritization of the important task to be postponed? Alternatively, do you find yourself thinking, "It is acceptable to defer this task for a later time, as I can prioritize and engage in an alternative activity for the present moment."?

This is called procrastination. It is an acquired proficiency, albeit not one that you particularly aspire to enhance.

What is Procrastination?

Procrastination can be described as the act of postponing or delaying something to a later time, or choosing to defer it.

Why do People Procrastinate?

Procrastination occurs due to a multitude of factors. Occasionally, individuals may exhibit reluctance due to their lack of desire, uncertainty about their intended course of action, or preference for avoidance. Some individuals may lack the know-how to undertake the task, while others who are perfectionists may find themselves constrained by time constraints or impatience, preventing them from completing it to their desired standards.

Avoiding Procrastination

If one encounters the tendency to procrastinate in the face of an impending task, one should not lose hope, for there exist numerous strategies to aid oneself in such situations. Commence by attenuating all sources of distraction (as discussed in the preceding section), subsequently proceed with the implementation of the following straightforward procedures.

Reward Yourself

If one is aware of a delightful reward that awaits them afterwards, it can expedite the completion of a task that is otherwise deemed unsatisfactory. Consider prioritizing the completion of unpleasant tasks during the morning hours to effectively eliminate them from your to-do list and minimize the likelihood of time constraints preventing their completion later in the day.

More Often

If you encounter assignments that you would prefer to postpone for various reasons, endeavor to complete them with greater frequency. For instance, if a task is designated for completion on a weekly basis, consider increasing its frequency to three or four occurrences.

By adhering to this approach, you will encounter greater difficulty in succumbing to procrastination, as you will be aware of the impending need to complete the task.

Create a Memorandum for Your Personal Reference

At one juncture or another, we tend to overlook certain tasks. Research indicates that the act of transcribing thoughts onto paper substantially enhances the chances of accomplishing them. If you do not possess a fondness for documenting information or occasionally find it difficult to keep track of physical records, it is advisable to orally communicate your plans to someone trusted. Being aware of someone else's knowledge regarding your tasks can serve as a source of motivation, as you can request their assistance in monitoring your progress to ensure successful completion.

Seeking assistance from someone

Engaging in collaborative efforts can serve as an effective strategy for overcoming procrastination. As an illustration, should you desire to visit the gym yet frequently lack the impetus to do so, kindly make a request to accompany you by a companion. This can also prove beneficial in a professional setting, particularly when there is a project to be completed. The desire to avoid disappointing others can serve as a powerful source of motivation on certain occasions.

It is imperative to engage in self-reflection and maintain genuine sincerity towards oneself.

Have you considered whether it would be advantageous to defer this? And concluded that the answer is affirmative? I bet you haven't. Pondering this inquiry serves as an excellent means of motivating oneself to accomplish various tasks, be it contacting one's insurance agent, communicating with one's child's school, or reaching out to one's employer. If the response is anything other than affirmative, there is absolutely no justification for postponing it.

After It's Completed

Certain tasks may not be inherently enjoyable, irrespective of the embellishment surrounding them. However, a profound sense of satisfaction will inevitably be derived upon their completion. Consider this, you will have the opportunity to satisfactorily mark off the corresponding item on your agenda and proceed towards a significantly more enjoyable undertaking. Rather than directing your attention towards the tasks at hand, prioritize your focus on the ultimate outcome. Consider the sentiments that arise when you gaze down upon the Checklist and discover that every item has been successfully marked as completed. Please bear this in mind when you detect the onset of procrastination.

Prepare the Groundwork

For larger tasks, it is advisable to approach them in manageable segments. Breaking a large task into smaller, manageable segments can significantly enhance its tolerability. As an illustration, in the event that you are tasked with composing a significant report for your supervisor, commence by seeking out appropriate online resources to facilitate your research. Subsequently, evaluate the duration you anticipate requiring to conduct extensive research and compose a comprehensive report. Subsequently, meticulously allocate that period in your planner or schedule, and make certain that there are no other engagements or obligations that could potentially divert your attention from the assigned task, such as a prior engagement or scheduled event. Now that you have completed the task in smaller sections, you will discover that it becomes more manageable.

The Consequences

An alternative approach to addressing procrastination involves reminding oneself of the potential ramifications associated with not undertaking the task at hand. Positive thinking can undoubtedly serve as a powerful source of encouragement, yet conversely, experiencing loss can yield comparable results. As an illustration, indulging in a chocolate bar and a glass of wine may provide temporary respite while tackling a pile of reports, however, facing unemployment and financial insolvency can deliver comparable outcomes in this regard.

Finding your Own Way

Procrastination is a phenomenon that affects individuals in various facets of their lives, encompassing both personal and professional domains. The key to effectively managing this tendency lies in identifying the most suitable strategies for one's own circumstances.

Goals necessitate diligent effort and effective time allocation.

The accomplishment of any individual objective necessitates diligent effort and the implementation of well-organized temporal arrangements to coalesce seamlessly with the purpose of realizing our aspirations. When altering a course of action to align with your objective, it is imperative to implement an effective and consistent time management strategy. I will be providing an illustration of an ineffective time management strategy and an ambitiously unrealistic goal agreement:

As stated by Business Week Online, the process of declaring bankruptcy is anticipated to be more arduous than ever before. Legal professionals suggest that addressing your bankruptcies at present can alleviate potential complications in the future. According to statistical data, a considerable number of individuals are resorting to filing for bankruptcy, while there is also a notable influx of business owners and other parties approaching the court for similar purposes. If this is not your objective, there is no cause for concern. However, in the absence of a meticulously planned time management strategy, you might belong to the category of individuals highlighted in a publication like Business Week Online, grappling with the repercussions of filing for bankruptcy in the future.

Do you consider this objective to be part of your long-term aspirations over the course of the upcoming decade? If not, it would be advisable for you to begin dedicating yourself to fulfilling the necessary obligations, such as putting in diligent work and exerting considerable effort, to effectively pursue your objectives. The passage of time eludes our grasp, and in the absence of vigilant time management, both time and money are irretrievably squandered, with no possibility of reversal. In the present day, the achievement of a singular objective necessitates the collaboration of two individuals. Nevertheless, in the event that we are unattached, the potential to progress with a lower degree of exertion may be underestimated. A viable illustration would be to prioritize completing your tasks promptly as a means of reducing the amount of time invested.

Alternatively, you have the option to make a prudent choice and obtain employment that offers a salary commensurate with your skills and qualifications. There exists a multitude of choices in relation to time management, and no decision should be disregarded or omitted. Over the span of a decade, various unforeseen events may transpire. We have the ability to formulate a meticulously designed strategy that appears impervious, but unforeseen circumstances arise when we fail to account for all facets of existence within that strategy. Presently, the incidence of bankruptcies frequently stems from a lack of attentiveness towards effective time management. It is probable that certain individuals had overlooked the inclusion of unforeseen events and proper allocation of time in their management strategy, whereas others might have underestimated their accomplishments and indulged in excessive spending. Regardless of the cause, it appears that an individual failed to implement effective work and time management.

When strategically devising a plan to accomplish our objectives, it is crucial that we first introspect and subsequently address other necessary factors that contribute to the attainment of our goals. Gaining self-awareness prior to assessing our strengths and weaknesses can enable us to identify any deficiencies and determine the facet of our being that is most dominant. Time management strategies aid individuals in achieving their objectives by instilling and sustaining motivation. If we find ourselves lacking in motivation (sustaining motivation during the course of pursuing our objective requires effort), we must seek a resolution. Commencing with acquiring self-awareness serves as the initial stride towards establishing objectives, attaining them, and establishing an efficacious time management system.

After overcoming this obstacle, our subsequent step will involve devising a strategy to effectively achieve our objectives. We embark on a journey of both diligent labor and astute cognition. Education, being one of the most invaluable resources, serves as a guiding beacon towards triumph. If you possess deficiencies in education and skills, and your objective appears impractical, it is evident that self-improvement is necessary. Commencing a business endeavor is always accompanied by considerable challenges and complexities. It necessitates a significant investment of time, exertion, and financial resources. If one does not possess these three essential components, their objective can be deemed unattainable. Consequently, it is imperative that you establish a meticulously crafted financial plan, including budgeting, savings allocation, and meticulous time management, in order to successfully meet your anticipated objectives. There exists a multitude of methods to generate income and accumulate savings.

"All that is required is the acquisition of knowledge, the development of skills, and the commitment to accomplish our goals." Now, upon examination of the visual representation accompanying this article, it can be inferred that in the forthcoming decade, should one wish to avoid entanglement with legal proceedings in order to declare insolvency, it would be prudent to initiate proactive measures promptly and engage in diligent daily efforts. Concurrently, meticulous formulation of a strategic blueprint that facilitates the achievement of one's objectives is strongly advised.

Chapter Six: Establishing a Timetable and Adhering to It

Schedules can greatly facilitate one's daily life. You have the option of employing a calendar, leveraging your smartphone, or simply resorting to a notebook. Every single individual who has achieved remarkable success maintains a meticulously organized agenda. This is the utmost essential requirement that you must possess. Schedules are instrumental in assisting individuals in effectively managing time by maintaining a record of completed tasks and upcoming responsibilities.

When you acquire obligations, ensure to promptly incorporate them into your schedule. Through the adoption of this approach, one can effectively discern and allocate available time for alternative pursuits. Ensure that you engage in proactive planning when organizing your schedule, allowing sufficient time to transit between various events or appointments. If there is a time gap of 20 minutes between your consecutive appointments, and it requires 30 minutes for you to commute to the second one, it is evident that the allocated time is insufficient.

Calendars offer the advantage of being conveniently displayed either on a wall or a desk surface. When an individual places a call or when an appointment needs to be scheduled, one simply needs to consult the aforementioned source. Additionally, it proves beneficial to have other individuals residing in your household who also have scheduling requirements. It proves to be greatly advantageous should you be required to accompany them to these appointments or other engagements. This is an item that you will encounter on a daily basis, thereby making it more difficult for it to slip from your memory. Furthermore, it increases the difficulty for individuals to manage conflicting commitments.

Mobile devices invariably come equipped with calendar functions. One can input data into these systems to effectively monitor and manage one's schedule on a daily, weekly, or even monthly basis. One can also incorporate alarms and reminders within the calendar to effectively adhere to the schedule. It possesses the capacity to serve as an exceptional resource in terms of time management. This proves to be particularly advantageous for individuals who are under medication. One can establish alarms to ensure timely and consistent administration of the medication.

Computers also have calendars. This would be highly beneficial for individuals who engage in extensive computer-related tasks due to professional commitments. You simply need to retrieve it and review the plans you have made.

If there are no other alternatives, you have the option of documenting a schedule in a notebook. This can be beneficial as a supplementary tool to a physical calendar or a mobile device. If one does not have immediate access to their calendar, computer, or a charged phone, it would be advantageous to possess a notebook as a reliable contingency. Small ones can be found at nearly every retail establishment. You have the option to store it conveniently in your pocket, vehicle, desk, or handbag to ensure effortless retrieval.

Please find below a sample of a daily itinerary:

7 o'clock in the morning - partake in the morning meal.

At 8 o'clock in the morning, proceed to the post office for the purpose of collecting a parcel.

Appointment scheduled at Kelly's Salon for 9:15am, with a duration of 1 hour.

10:45am – retrieve garments from the dry cleaners "10:45am – collect dry cleaning items

At 11:20am, I have a scheduled meeting with Erin at Sam's Deli for a duration of one hour.

12:45pm - proceed to the fitness center

Commence work at 2:00pm for a duration of 4 hours.

professional commitments. You simply need to retrieve it and review the plans you have made.

If there are no other alternatives, you have the option of documenting a schedule in a notebook. This can be beneficial as a supplementary tool to a physical calendar or a mobile device. If one does not have immediate access to their calendar, computer, or a charged phone, it would be advantageous to possess a notebook as a reliable contingency. Small ones can be found at nearly every retail establishment. You have the option to store it conveniently in your pocket, vehicle, desk, or handbag to ensure effortless retrieval.

Please find below a sample of a daily itinerary:

7 o'clock in the morning - partake in the morning meal.

At 8 o'clock in the morning, proceed to the post office for the purpose of collecting a parcel.

Appointment scheduled at Kelly's Salon for 9:15am, with a duration of 1 hour.

10:45am – retrieve garments from the dry cleaners "10:45am – collect dry cleaning items

At 11:20am, I have a scheduled meeting with Erin at Sam's Deli for a duration of one hour.

12:45pm - proceed to the fitness center

Commence work at 2:00pm for a duration of 4 hours.

Return to residence at 6:00pm and prepare an evening meal.

8:00pm – allocate time for personal rejuvenation

9:00pm – Indulge in personal hygiene and retire to bed

Should you have a preference for utilizing a weekly timetable, it would yield nearly identical results.

Please find below an illustrative representation of a weekly schedule:

Monday - scheduled a meeting with Erin at Sam's Deli for a lunch appointment at 11:20am.

On Tuesday, there is a scheduled medical appointment at 10:15am, followed by Billy's soccer game at 6:00pm, where it would be appreciated if you could bring refreshments.

On Wednesday, it is necessary to perform the task of placing the trashcan at curbside before the commencement of work. Additionally, at 4:00pm, it is imperative to collect the dry cleaning.

Thursday - Contact the newspaper to inquire about subscription renewal (preferably after 9am).

Friday - Escort Kelly to Angela's residence for an overnight stay at 5:00pm, Attend a dinner reception hosted by the Sanders family at 7:00pm.

Saturday – Free day

On Sunday, at 10:45am, I will retrieve Kelly from Angela's residence, followed by engaging in finger painting activities with the children for the entire afternoon.

Precision is not mandatory. One can provide approximate times for most activities, except in the case of a predetermined appointment. The objective is to establish a framework for your daily activities and ensure that you are aware of your leisure time, thus allowing you to allocate it effectively. Additionally, you have the option of dissecting larger tasks into smaller, more manageable components, thereby enabling you to allocate them throughout the course of the day, should that prove to be a more efficient strategy for you. The magnitude of a substantial project can become burdensome when considering the prospect of undertaking it in its entirety. If feasible, engaging in partial completion followed by temporary interruptions before resuming would attenuate the perception of the task's magnitude.

Devise a structured timetable, considering your optimal periods during the day. Are you a morning person? Subsequently, arrange the most challenging tasks to be completed during the morning. Do you tend to perform more effectively during afternoon hours? In that case, that period ought to be the time during which you are occupied. Furthermore, it should be acknowledged that there will invariably be certain instances where delays or unanticipated complications arise. You may be required to make modifications either by eliminating certain commitments or incorporating new ones into your schedule. Demonstrate adaptability and everything will turn out well. However, adhering to a schedule can alleviate the stress if unforeseen circumstances arise.

www.ingramcontent.com/pod-product-compliance
Lightning Source LLC
Chambersburg PA
CBHW071124130526
44590CB00056B/1912